FOOTBALL SU

RASHFORD RULES

Hi, pleased to meet you.

We hope you enjoy our book about Marcus Rashford!

I'm VARbot with all the facts and stats!

THIS IS A WELBECK CHILDREN'S BOOK
Published in 2021 by Welbeck Children's Books Limited
An imprint of the Welbeck Publishing Group
20 Mortimer Street, London W1T 3JW

ISBN: 978-1-78312-866-2

Writer: Simon Mugford
Designer and Illustrator: Dan Green
Design manager: Sam James
Executive editor: Suhel Ahmed
Production: Arlene Alexander

A catalogue record for this book is available from the British Library.

Printed in the UK
10 9 8 7 6 5 4 3 2 1

Statistics and records correct as of June 2021

CHAPTER 1
MEET
MARCUS

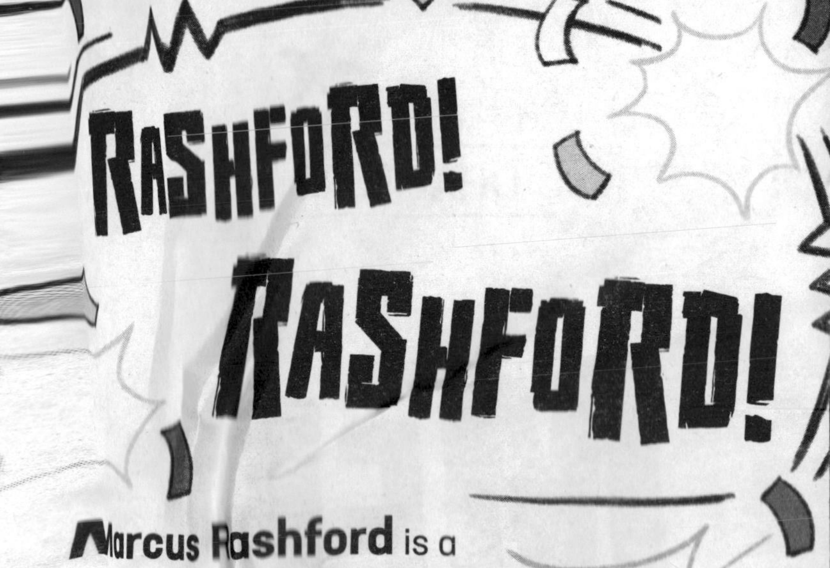
RASHFORD!
RASHFORD!

Marcus Rashford is a

BRILLIANT FOOTBALLER

who scores fantastic goals for

Manchester United and **England.**

AND . . . campaigning for charity made him a national hero.

Marcus is a **role model** for millions of people and this book is all about **him!**

WHAT MAKES RASHFORD SO AWESOME?

Speed
He makes very fast, direct runs into the box.

Height and strength
He's tall and strong – able to shake off defenders.

Shooting
Never afraid to take a shot on goal.

Vision
Can spot a great pass to open up defences.

GOALS!

MARCUS scores plenty of **GOALS, ESPECIALLY WHEN IT MATTERS.**

RASHFORD
is a superb
goalscorer and
team-player.
And he's a nice guy, too!

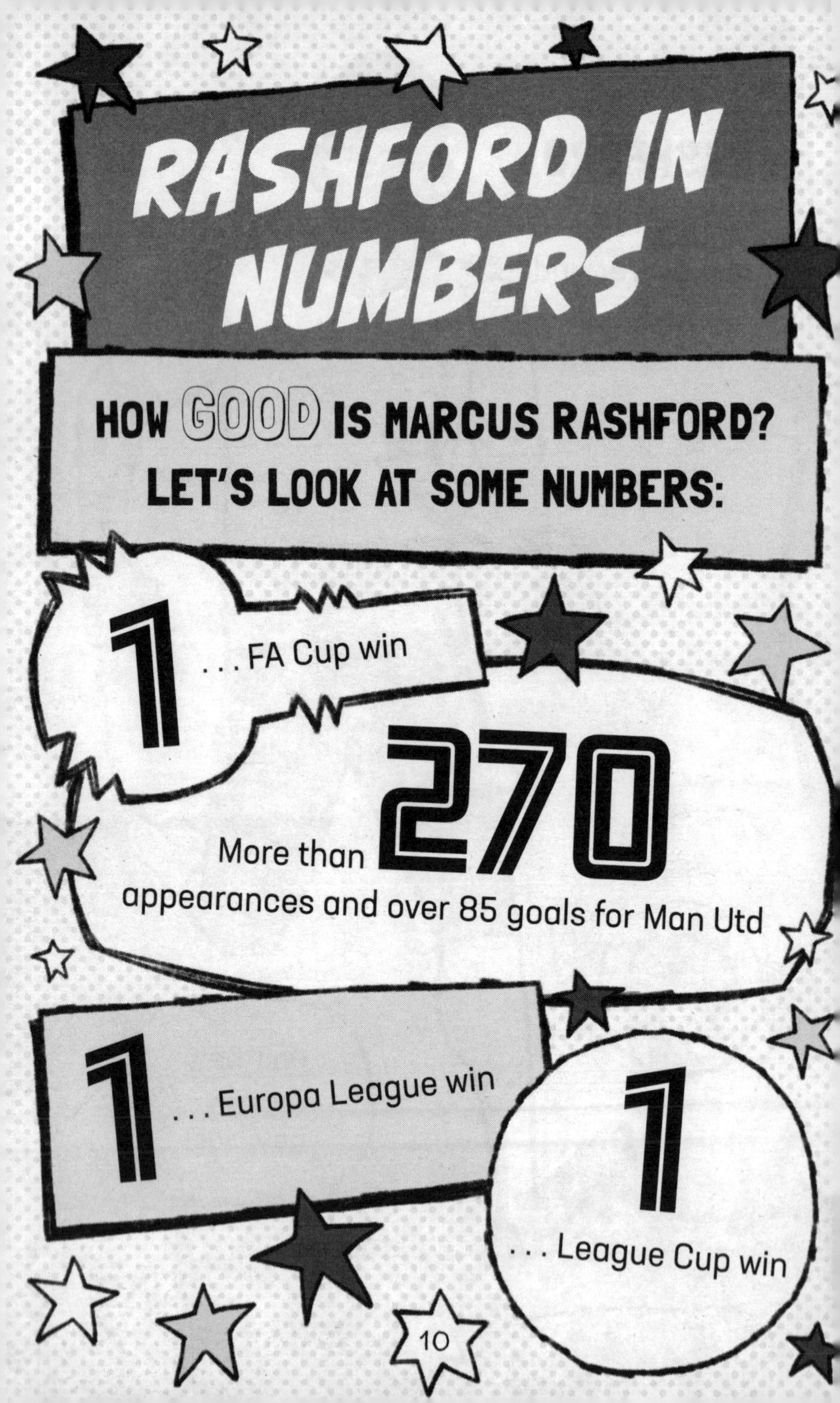
RASHFORD IN NUMBERS
HOW GOOD IS MARCUS RASHFORD? LET'S LOOK AT SOME NUMBERS:
1 . . . FA Cup win
More than 270 appearances and over 85 goals for Man Utd
1 . . . Europa League win
1 . . . League Cup win

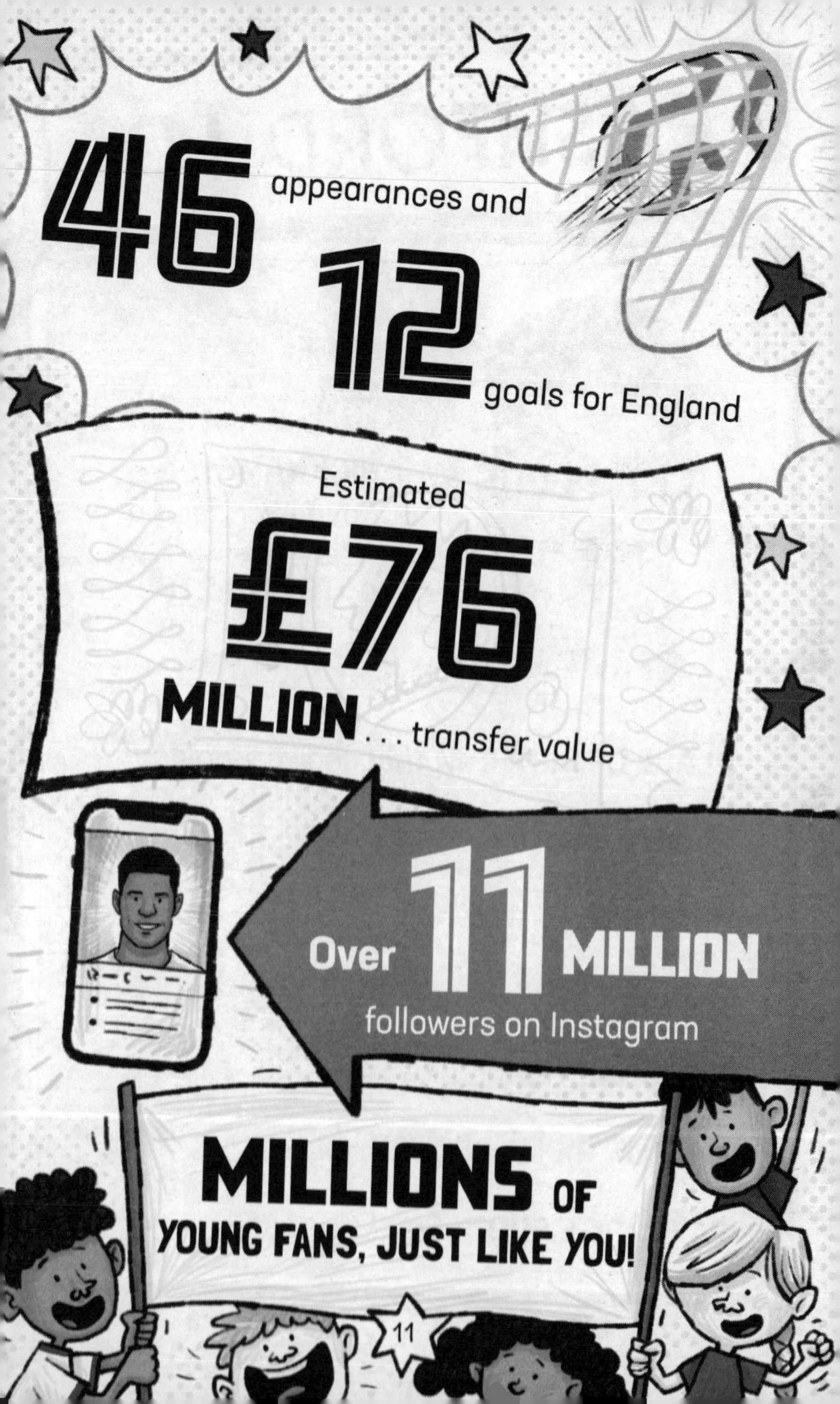
46 appearances and
12 goals for England
Estimated
£76
MILLION . . . transfer value
Over 11 MILLION
followers on Instagram
MILLIONS OF
YOUNG FANS, JUST LIKE YOU!

RASHFORD I.D.

NAME:
Marcus Rashford

NICKNAME:
Rash, Wonder Kid

DATE OF BIRTH:
31 October 1997

PLACE OF BIRTH: *Wythenshawe, England*

HEIGHT: *1.85 m*

POSITION: *Forward*

CLUBS: *Manchester United*

NATIONAL TEAM: *England*

LEFT OR RIGHT-FOOTED: *Right*

FAVOURITE FOOD: *Breakfast cereal*

CHAPTER 2

MANCHESTER BOY

Marcus Rashford was born in **1997** in **Wythenshawe,** on the outskirts of Manchester.

If she was stil
school, ther
family nearb

SLURP!

The **Manchester United** stadium,
Old Trafford, is just a few miles away.

GLORY, GLORY, MAN UNITED!

Manchester United were the Premier League Champions in 1997.

When he was six, Marcus began training at a local club called **Fletcher Moss Rangers,** where his dad was a coach.

These players also started

out at **Fletcher Moss:**

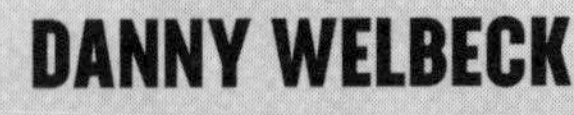

When he was **FIVE,** Marcus went to **Old Trafford** for the first time. United were playing **Real Madrid** in the **Champions League quarter-final.**

WOW!
WHAT A MATCH!

Madrid's star striker **Ronaldo** scored an incredible hat-trick. United were knocked out, but the **Old Trafford** crowd **applauded** Ronaldo as he left the pitch.

Ronaldo looked different back then.
Not *THAT* Ronaldo!
RONALDO

Ronaldo was Marcus' **hero.** He wanted to be just like the Real Madrid star.

CHAPTER 3
WONDER
KID

At **Fletcher Moss**, Marcus scored lots of goals.

Some very **big clubs** wanted to sign him up.

He said **NO**
to **Everton.**

And an extra big **NO** to **Liverpool**.

28 FEBRUARY 2016

PREMIER LEAGUE

MAN UTD 3-2 ARSENAL

Just **three days** after his amazing debut, Marcus lined up with his team-mates to face **Arsenal,** in one of the biggest fixtures in the **Premier League.**

AND GUESS WHAT?

HE SCORED AGAIN!

TWO goals in **THREE** minutes, plus an **assist** for the third goal.

Marcus was **Man of the Match** - again - and **definitely** the man of the moment.

PREMIER LEAGUE

MAN CITY 0-1 MAN UTD

Another massive game – the **Manchester Derby.** United had not beaten City in an away match for **FOUR** years. **Marcus** was ready to **change that!**

After 16 minutes, Marcus picked up a pass from **Juan Mata,** ran into the box and –

THE BALL WAS IN THE BACK OF THE NET!

Marcus is the youngest United player to score in a Manchester Derby.

Marcus scored a superb goal against **West Ham** in the sixth round of **the FA Cup.** United went on to beat **Crystal Palace** 2-1 in the final which brought Rashford a winner's medal in his debut season.

AMAZING!

RASHFORD'S 2015-16 RECORD

APPEARANCES	GOALS	ASSISTS
18	8	2

"I SEE SOME OF MYSELF IN HIM FOR SURE. HE HAS COURAGE AND HE'S FAST AND IS VERY GOOD WITH THE BALL."

Ronaldo, legendary Brazilian striker

Rashford's ***all-time hero,*** remember!

CHAPTER 6

YOUNG LION

The **England** coaches wanted Marcus in their team, so he was selected for the **UEFA EURO 2016** tournament in **France.**

But first, there was a **warm-up match** to play . . .

27 MAY 2016

INTERNATIONAL FRIENDLY

ENGLAND 2-1 AUSTRALIA

This was Rashford's **first senior game** for England – only four months after his United debut. Did he score? Of course he did – after just **three minutes!**

WHOOSH!

Marcus is the youngest England player to score on his debut.
He would also be the youngest England player at the EUROS!

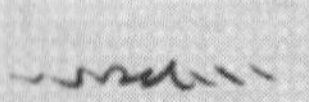

EURO 2016

In the end, England didn't play that well at **Euro 2016.**

YOU MEAN THEY WERE **RUBBISH!**
ENGLAND FANS

They were **knocked out** of the tournament after **losing 2–1** to **Iceland.** Many people said **Marcus** was the **best England player** that night - and he only played for the last **four minutes!**

* Iceland was home to the Vikings

HAT-TRICK HERO

6 SEPTEMBER 2016

ENGLAND U-21 6-1 NORWAY U-21

Marcus made his debut for the England under-21s **AFTER** he'd played for the senior side!

And this being Rashford, he scored again!

But not once, or even twice - he scored

THREE times for a **hat-trick.**

So, 2016 was pretty good for Marcus:

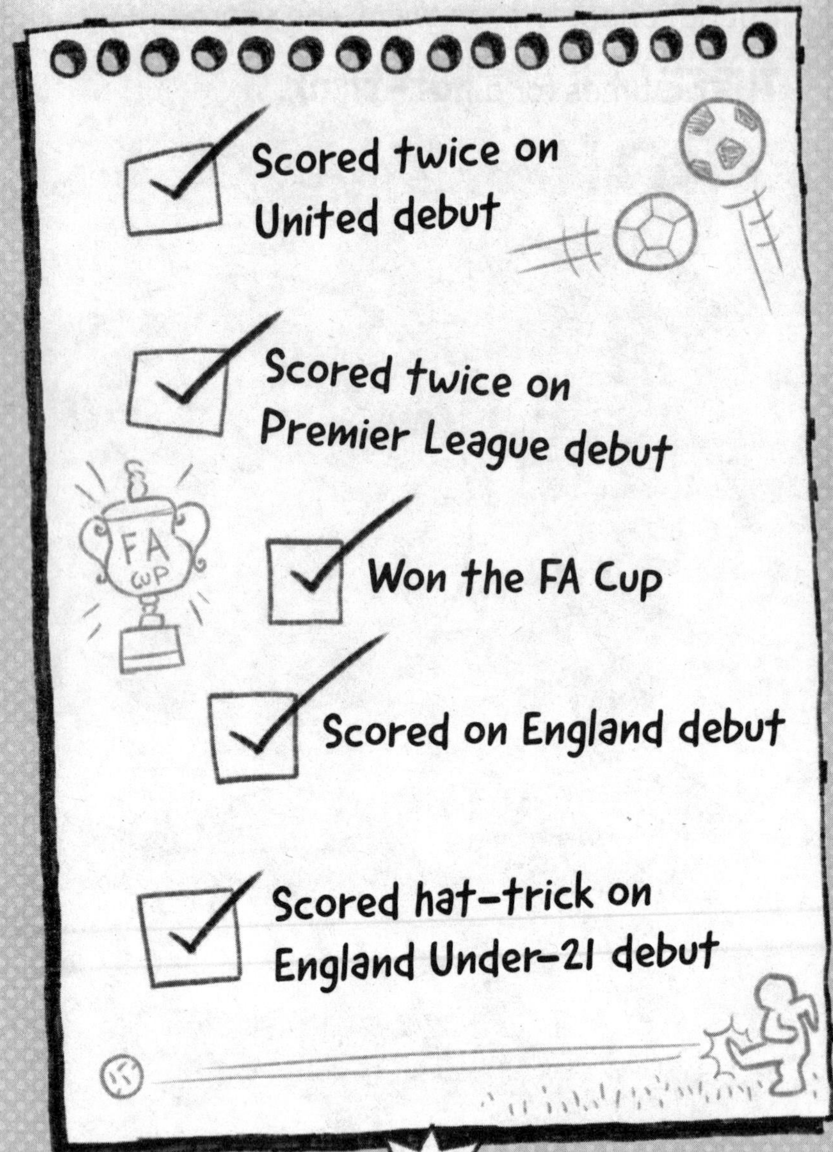

Scored twice on United debut
Scored twice on Premier League debut
FA CUP
Won the FA Cup
Scored on England debut
Scored hat-trick on England Under-21 debut

CHAPTER 7

HEAD TO HEAD

THE 200 CLUB

In **January 2020**, Marcus played his **200th** game for **Manchester United.**

Marcus scored twice!

Rashford is the **fourth-youngest** United player to make 200 appearances.

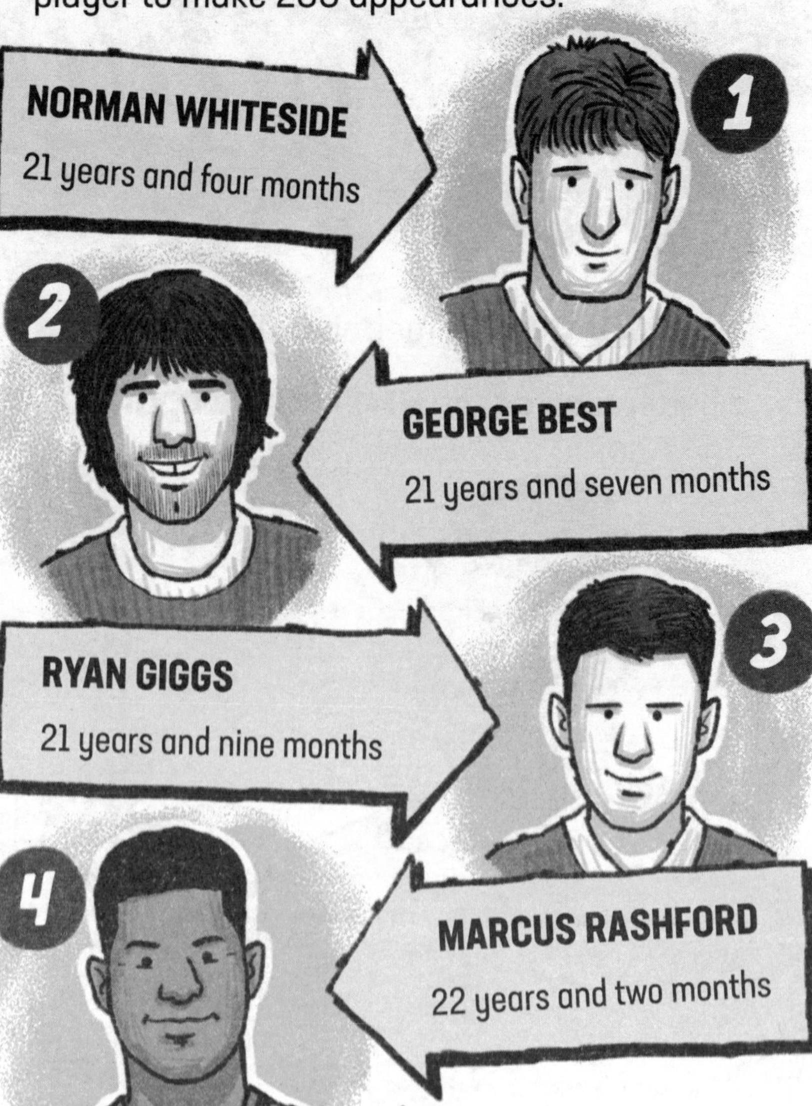

RASH VERSUS RONALDO

After **200 games** for United, Rashford had a better record than **Cristiano Ronaldo.**

RASHFORD

GOALS

64

STARTS

137

MINUTES PER GOAL

200

RONALDO

GOALS

54

STARTS

159

MINUTES PER GOAL

272

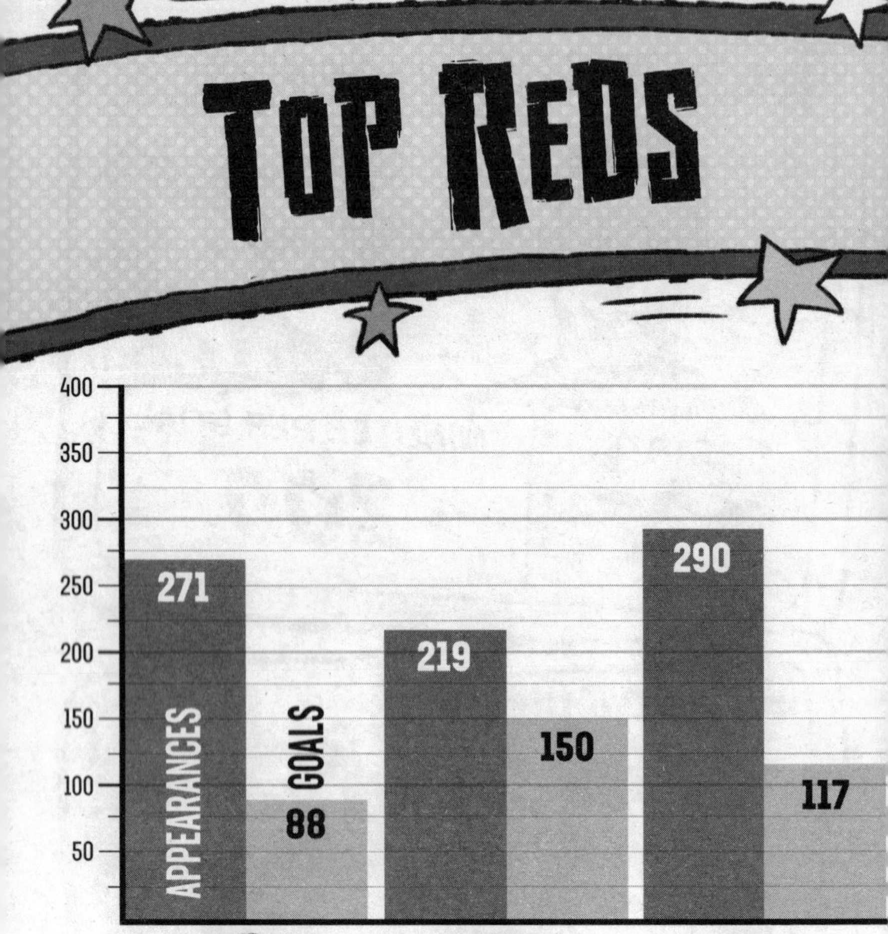

MARCUS RASHFORD
2016-

RUUD VAN NISTELROOY
2001-2006

CRISTIANO RONALDO
2003-2009

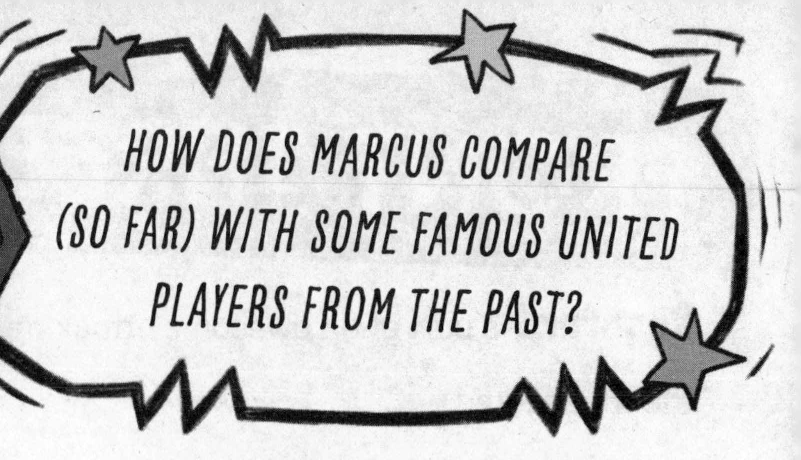

HOW DOES MARCUS COMPARE (SO FAR) WITH SOME FAMOUS UNITED PLAYERS FROM THE PAST?

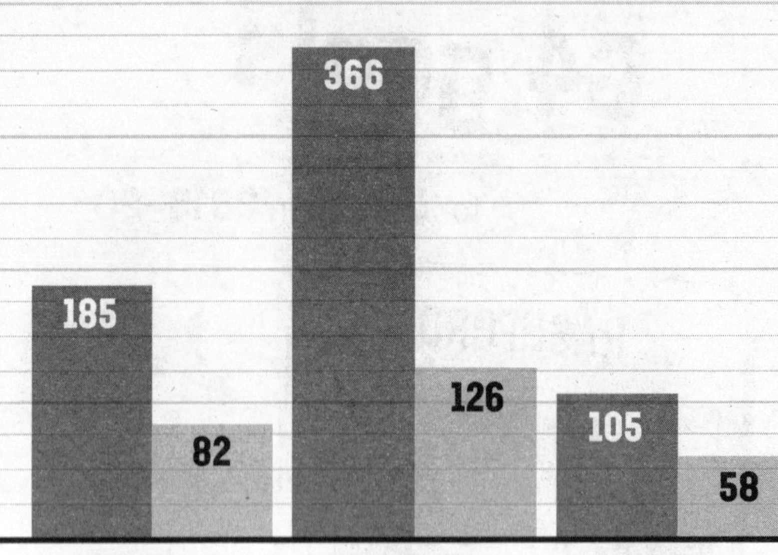

185
82
366
126
105
58

ERIC CANTONA
1992-1997

OLE GUNNER SOLSKJAER
1996-2007

ROBIN VAN PERSIE
2012-2015

FRONT THREE

Rashford is part of an awesome attacking trio that scored

64 goals

for **United** in **2019–20.**

ANTHONY MARTIAL
23 Goals
MASON GREENWOOD
19 Goals
Liverpool's Mo Salah, Sadio Mané and Roberto Firmino only managed 57 goals.

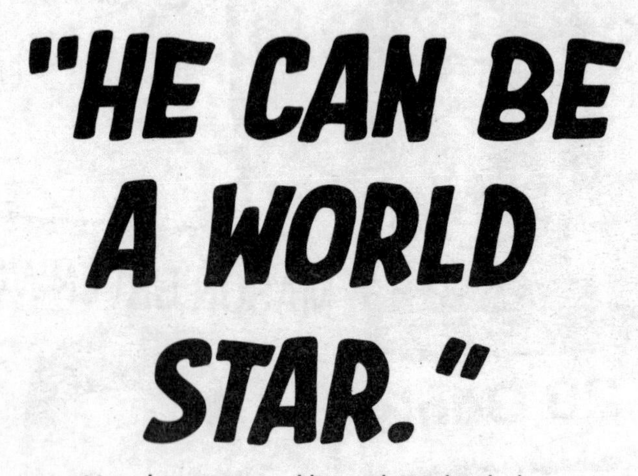
"HE CAN BE A WORLD STAR."
Manchester United legend, Paul Scholes

CHAPTER 8

MARCUS MAGIC

By the start of the **2016–17** season, Manchester United had a new manager – **José Mourinho.**

And Marcus swapped his **number 39** shirt for **number 19.**

United kicked off the season by winning the **Community Shield.**

Mourinho had signed Swedish super striker **Zlatan Ibrahimović.**

Marcus moved out to the **left wing**, while **Zlatan** played as the **centre-forward.**

In February 2017, United won the **League Cup** to bring Rashford trophy number **THREE.**

United beat
Southampton 3-2.

2016-17 HIGHLIGHTS

THE BEST BITS OF RASHFORD'S FIRST FULL SEASON IN THE UNITED FIRST TEAM.

27 AUGUST 2016

PREMIER LEAGUE

HULL CITY 0-1 MAN UTD

Rashford *came on for* ***Juan Mata*** *in the 71st minute of this goalless match. His injury-time* ***winning goal*** *was his first of the season.*

21 SEPTEMBER 2016

LEAGUE CUP THIRD ROUND

NORTHAMPTON TOWN 1-3 MAN UTD

*Marcus was the **super-sub** again, coming on to provide an assist for the **second goal,** scored by Ander Herrera, before scoring the **third.***

20 APRIL 2017

EUROPA LEAGUE QUARTER-FINAL 2ND LEG

MAN UTD 2-1 ANDERLECHT

*Marcus was again involved in both goals, assisting **one** and **scoring the other** to seal an important win in extra-time!*

CHAMPION!
24 MAY 2017
UEFA EUROPA LEAGUE FINAL
AJAX 0-2 MAN UTD
Marcus had his first taste of European success with United as they beat Ajax to win the Europa League in Stockholm.

IT WAS HIS **FOURTH** TROPHY WITH UNITED!

RASHFORD'S 2016-17 RECORD

APPEARANCES	GOALS	ASSISTS
53	11	7

Rashford played more games for United than any other player this season!

...58, 59, 60, 61, 62, 63...

BALLbot counting keepy-uppies

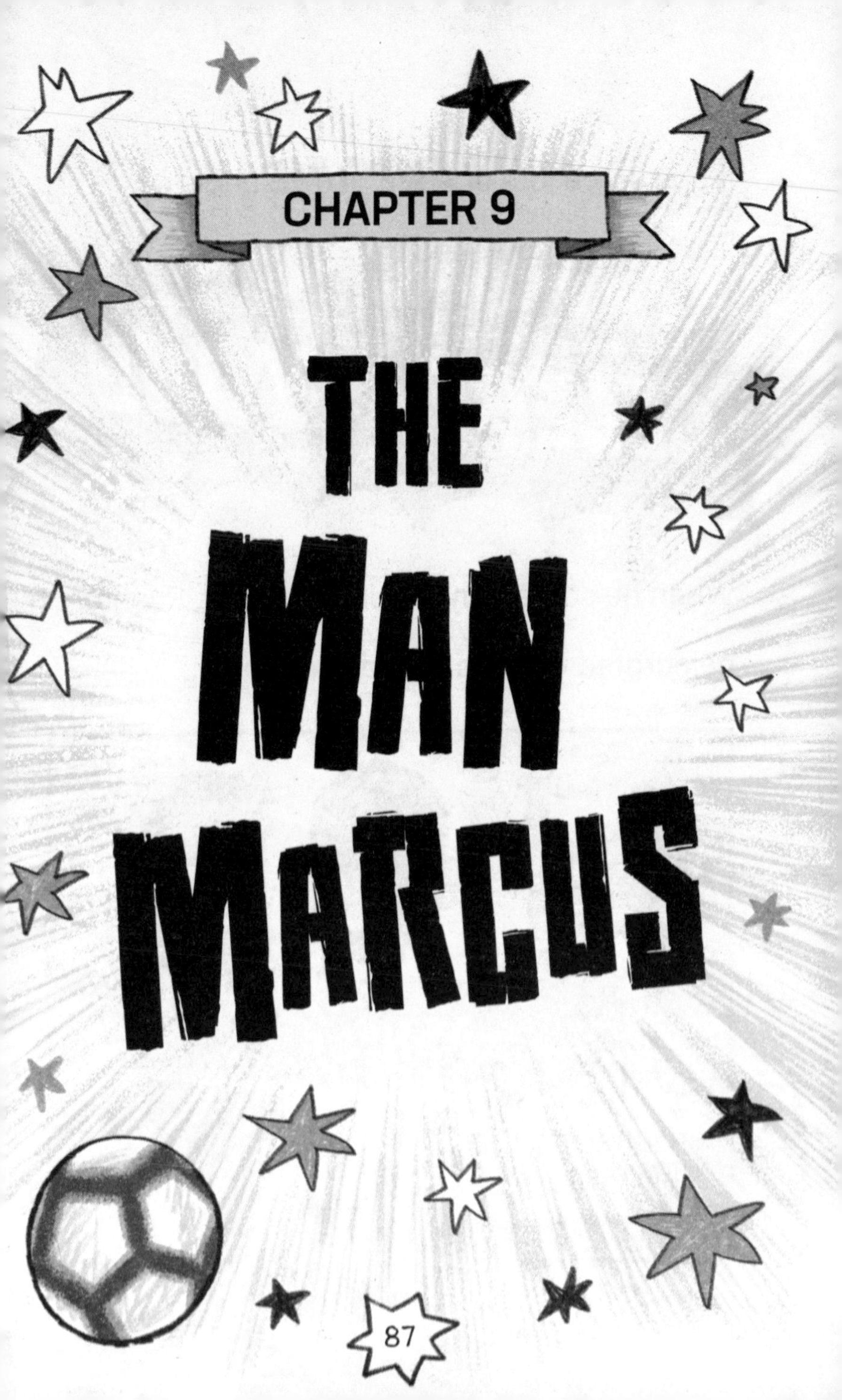

CHAPTER 9

THE MAN MARCUS

If you score lots of ***AWESOME*** goals

like Marcus, you need a

CELEBRATION!

When he scored on his United debut, Rashford celebrated with his friends and family.

A BIG LEAP IN THE AIR
ALWAYS LOOKS GOOD!

MARCUS MUST-HAVES

Ever since he was a boy, Marcus has ***ALWAYS*** had a ball with him.

His dog, **Saint** goes everywhere with him (except on the pitch)!

2017-18 HIGHLIGHTS

ANOTHER BIG SEASON AT UNITED FOR MARCUS.

12 SEPTEMBER 2017

CHAMPIONS LEAGUE GROUP STAGE

MAN UTD 3-0 FC BASEL

It was Rashford's debut in the ***Champions League****, so he scored of course!*

20 SEPTEMBER 2017

LEAGUE CUP THIRD ROUND

MAN UTD 4-1 BURTON ALBION

*Marcus scored **TWO** early goals and assisted **Anthony Martial** for another!*

10 MARCH 2018

PREMIER LEAGUE

MAN UTD 2-1 LIVERPOOL

*Rashford had been out of the **starting line-up** for a while, but what a way to come back! **TWO** goals against **MASSIVE** rivals **Liverpool!***

RASHFORD'S 2017-18 RECORD

APPEARANCES	GOALS	ASSISTS
52	13	10

CHAPTER 10

THE ENGLAND MAN

4 SEPTEMBER 2017

WORLD CUP QUALIFIER

ENGLAND 2-1 SLOVAKIA

This was a **BIG** game for **England.** Marcus made a **mistake** which led to Slovakia taking an early lead. **OH NO!** Eric Dier made it **1-1** and then in the second half . . .

POW!

Rashford fired into the net from long-range.

He'd scored for **England** at **Wembley!**

HOW AWESOME IS THAT?

Marcus was in
the squad for the
WORLD CUP
in RUSSIA.
19
WHAT AN
AMAZING
HONOUR!

With lots of players **under 25,** England had one of the **youngest squads** at the tournament.

Marcus made his **World Cup debut** as a substitute in England's first game against Tunisia.

He was so proud.

And so was his mum!

The game against **Colombia** went to a **penalty shoot-out.** This was a **BIG DEAL.** England had **never won** a **World Cup** penalty shoot-out.

I can't watch!

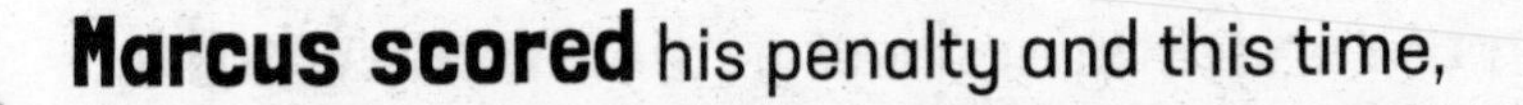

Marcus scored his penalty and this time,

ENGLAND WON!

The **whole** country went

CRAZY with **excitement.**

YAY!

ENGERRLAND!
ENGERRLAND!

In the end, England lost in the **semi-finals**, but it was their best World Cup for **28 years.** Marcus and his team-mates played **brilliantly.**

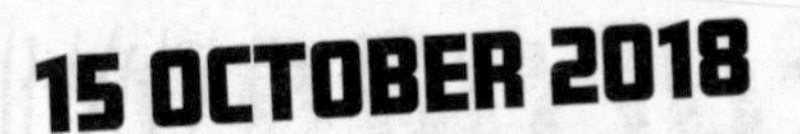

15 OCTOBER 2018

NATIONS LEAGUE GROUP STAGE

SPAIN 2-3 ENGLAND

Marcus had a fantastic game, scoring **one goal** and assisting **Raheem Sterling** for another, as **England beat Spain** in this new tournament.

RASHFORD'S ENGLAND RECORD

CAPS	GOALS	ASSISTS
38	10	6

CONGRATULATIONS, VARBOT. A NEW PERSONAL BEST. 3 MILLION KEEPY-UPPIES!

CHAPTER 11
NUMBER
10

In **2018**, Marcus was given the **Number 10** shirt after **Zlatan Ibrahimović** left United.

That shirt has been worn by some VERY famous names at the club.
SHERINGHAM 10
V.NISTELROOY 10
Are you going to help me with these?
ROONEY 10

Despite the new shirt, Rashford failed to score early in the **2018–19 season.** And then he picked up a **red card!**

In December, United legend **Ole Gunnar Solskjaer** took over from José Mourinho as manager. Marcus scored in Solskjaer's **first game** in charge and then scored **FOUR** goals in **FIVE** games!

6 MARCH 2019

UEFA CHAMPIONS LEAGUE LAST 16, 2ND LEG

PSG 1-3 MAN UTD

Penalty to United!

United were heading **OUT** of the **Champions League** when **VAR** (Video Assistant Referee) confirmed they had a penalty in injury time. Under enormous pressure, **super-cool** Rashford stepped up to take it . . . and ***BOOM!*** The ball went in the back of the net and United had won on away goals.

WHOOSH!

RASHFORD'S 2018-19 RECORD

APPEARANCES	GOALS	ASSISTS
47	13	9

2019-20 HIGHLIGHTS

A SEASON LIKE NO OTHER

11 AUGUST 2019

PREMIER LEAGUE

MAN UTD 4-0 CHELSEA

Rashford scored ***TWICE*** *against* ***Chelsea*** *in the opening game of the season.*

POW!

30 OCTOBER 2019

LEAGUE CUP FOURTH ROUND

CHELSEA 1-MAN UTD 2

Marcus scored another ***two goals*** *against the London club, including a* ***SCORCHER*** *of a long-range free-kick.* ***BOOM!***

4 DECEMBER 2019

PREMIER LEAGUE

MAN UTD 2-1 TOTTENHAM

Another London club and another **two goals.** One of **FOUR braces** for Marcus in the season.

Marcus was in brilliant form until he got **injured** in early **2020.**

And then in **March,** all football matches stopped because of the **Coronavirus pandemic.**

FOOTBALL SUPERSTARS NEWS
BREAKING NEWS
FOOTBALL is taking a break. Stay safe, everybody!
FOOTBALL CANCELLED

When matches started again in **June** (with no fans), Marcus had recovered from his injury and **started scoring** goals again!

RASHFORD'S 2019-20 RECORD

APPEARANCES	GOALS	ASSISTS
44	22	11

It was his best goalscoring season so far!
WANT TO DO SOME MORE KEEPY-UPPIES?

CHAPTER 12

NATIONAL TREASURE

Marcus has **never forgotten** the **community** he grew up in. It was a place where families like his had help with things such as **free school meals,** but they also **helped each other.**

WITHOUT THE KINDNESS AND GENEROSITY OF THE COMMUNITY I HAD AROUND ME, THERE WOULDN'T BE THE MARCUS RASHFORD YOU SEE TODAY.

In **2020,** Marcus worked with the charity **FareShare** to raise **£20 MILLION** for families in need.

During the **Coronavirus lockdown,** lots of people needed **extra help.** Families who received free school meals were given **food vouchers** while schools were closed.

When the **British government** planned to stop the vouchers, **Marcus spoke out.** He **wrote a letter** that was seen by millions of people on **social media.**

And **amazingly,** the **government** listened! They made the food vouchers available for the school holidays, too.

DAILY NEWS
FREE BARNARD CASTLE EYE TEST VOUCHER
GOVERNMENT U-TURN

The **brilliant young footballer** was now a **successful activist,** too.

QUIZ TIME!

How much do you know about Marcus Rashford? Try this quiz to find out, then test your friends!

1. Which trophy did Marcus win first with Manchester United?

---

2. Where was Marcus born?

---

3. What was the name of the local club that he played for?

---

4. Which Brazilian player was his hero?

5. How many goals did Rashford score on his United debut?

---

6. Which team did Marcus score against on his England debut?

---

7. How old was Rashford when he made his 200th United appearance?

---

8. Marcus scored for England in a World Cup penalty shoot-out. Which team were they playing against?

---

9. How many goals did Rashford score for United in 2019-20?

---

10. How much money did Marcus help raise for the charity, FareShare?

The answers are on the next page ***but no peeking!***

ANSWERS

1. The FA Cup
2. Wythenshawe (Manchester)
3. Fletcher Moss Rangers
4. Ronaldo
5. Two
6. Australia
7. 22 years, two months
8. Colombia
9. 22
10. £20 Million

MARCUS RASHFORD:
WORDS YOU NEED TO KNOW

Premier League
The top football league in England.

PFA
Professional Footballers' Association

FA Cup
The top English knockout cup competition.

VAR
Video Assistant Referee

UEFA Champions League
European club competition held every year. The winner is the best team in Europe.

UEFA Europa League
The second-tier European club competition.

Nations League
European national tournament that replaced some friendly matches.

ABOUT THE AUTHORS

Simon's first job was at the Science Museum, making paper aeroplanes and blowing bubbles big enough for your dad to stand in. Since then he's written all sorts of books about the stuff he likes, from dinosaurs and rockets, to llamas, loud music and of course, football. Simon has supported Ipswich Town since they won the FA Cup in 1978 (it's true - look it up) and once sat next to Rio Ferdinand on a train. He lives in Kent with his wife and daughter, two tortoises and a cat.

Dan has drawn silly pictures since he could hold a crayon. Then he grew up and started making books about stuff like trucks, space, people's jobs, *Doctor Who* and *Star Wars*. Dan remembers Ipswich Town winning the FA Cup but he didn't watch it because he was too busy making a Viking ship out of brown paper. As a result, he knows more about Vikings than football. Dan lives in Suffolk with his wife, son, daughter and a dog that takes him for very long walks.